The Smiling Athlete

17 Mindset Hacks & Tools to Master Mental Toughness, Strengthen Skills & Improve Your Grades!

PLUS - TIPS FROM THE PROS !

Baseball, Basketball, Football, Soccer, Track, Cheer & more!

SANDY COUCH BAIN   BOOK 1

Check out our website,

TheSmilingAthlete.com

to sign up and get lots of

free new hacks and tools personally emailed to you!

Also, **please leave an honest review on Amazon**
for this book, just a line or two. It would mean the world to
me. I personally read each review, and your feedback really
makes a difference! *Coach Bain*

 AMAZON REVIEW PAGE:
https://rebrand.ly/smilereview
◇◇◇◇◇

Citations, research studies, recommended books, etc. will be updated and added periodically at: TheSmilingAthlete.com.

ISBN 978-1-7376588-3-2

10 9 8 7 6 5 4 3 2 1

THE SMILING ATHLETE: CONTENTS

You've got this!

WHERE WERE YOU when you first felt like this? On a field, a court, or maybe a track? In a pool, a rink, or someplace else? Remember that sensation, the wind at your back, **feeling like an absolute superhero?** Your biggest worry was which after-game snack to choose!

It's different now, right? You're putting in effort, feeling the weight of pressure. Sometimes it's amazing. Other times...

But imagine recapturing that carefree magic again while **competing at a level higher than you ever thought possible**.

If you commit just 5 to 10 minutes a day *(to start)* to this book, **we can make it happen, together.**

With the hidden power within your mind and the hacks and tools in this book, you're fully equipped to embark on this quest. And **I'll be right there by your side, guiding you step by step**.

So, let's kick off this adventure by diving into the all-important Fundamental #1!

"You dream. You plan. You reach.
There will be obstacles.
There will be doubters.
There will be mistakes.
But with hard work, with belief,
with confidence and trust in yourself
and those around you,
there are no limits."

MICHAEL PHELPS (SWIMMING)
Most successful and most decorated Olympian
of all time with a total of 28 medals

the fundamentals

READ THIS FIRST!!!

MINDSET HACKS ARE EASY...
ONCE YOU LEARN THE FUNDAMENTALS!

PLEASE READ THIS FIRST!

*"Never say never
because limits, like fears,
are often just an illusion."*
MICHAEL JORDAN (BASKETBALL)

IF YOUR BRAIN CAN TELL YOUR BODY TO FEEL SCARED... CAN YOUR BRAIN TELL YOUR BODY TO FEEL BRAVE?

Fundamental #1

YOUR BRAIN DOES <u>NOT</u> KNOW THE DIFFERENCE BETWEEN WHAT'S REAL & WHAT YOU IMAGINE.

Do you ever watch scary movies? Assuming you've seen a few, what are some things that made you jump? Or made you feel like you couldn't breathe? Have you ever felt scared to the point that your stomach was so queasy, that you felt like you were going to throw up?

 How about this, have you ever had one of those times when you thought you lost your cell phone... but you really didn't? But in that moment, you completely freaked? Your heart started hammering against your chest. Because you believed in that instant... that you really did lose it?

What about a terrifying nightmare? The kind that's so scary that every muscle in your body screams at you to run, but you're frozen and can't move. Then you wake up, and for a moment, you still believe it's real? Have you ever had one of those?

Where did you feel the panic in your body?

I want you to remember back to one of those scary times and imagine it's happening now. Put your hand on the part of your body where you felt that fear or panic. For most people, it's their chest or stomach... or both.

So, even though the scary event wasn't real, like what happened in the movie, or the nightmare, or when you thought you lost your phone, your brain assumed it was real, so **it reacted as if it was real**.

1. Something that seems scary or threatening happens.

2. Whether it's real or not, your brain doesn't know the difference.

3. Your brain always assumes potential threats are real.

4. Your brain tells your body to react, as if the threat is real.

Write Your Answers or thoughts in the book!

Where do you feel panic in your body?

My brain always assumes potential threats are

_____.

DO THIS

What scares you? It doesn't matter if it seems stupid or makes no sense. It's real to you, and that's what matters.

*"Courage doesn't mean
you don't get afraid.
Courage means
you don't let fear stop you."*

BETHANY HAMILTON
(PROFESSIONAL SURFER
& SHARK ATTACK SURVIVOR)

*"I've never been afraid
of big moments.
I get butterflies. I get
nervous and anxious, but
I think those are all good
signs that I'm ready
for the moment."*

STEPHEN CURRY
(BASKETBALL)

*"Fear can be conquered.
I became a better person
and a better football player
when I learned that lesson."*

ROGER CRAIG (FOOTBALL)

Fundamental #2

LEARNING HOW TO USE YOUR FIGHT-OR-FLIGHT CHEMICALS WILL MAKE YOU A BETTER ATHLETE!

When your brain senses you're in immediate danger, like you're about to lose your life to a scary creature, or you think you lost your cell phone, your brain activates something called a fight-or-flight response. When this response is triggered, a bunch of chemicals flood into your body.

About 100,000 years ago, these chemicals saved the lives of many of our ancestors. Back then, Cousin Rocko had a very real chance of being eaten by saber toothed cats, giant hyenas, snakes, and cave bears... just to name a few.

Let's imagine that YOU are Cousin Rocko, one of our ancient relatives. Pretend you're just walking down the path, minding your own business, when all of a sudden, you see or hear a sign of danger. Maybe you notice a weird shadow. Or something moving in the trees or grass!

At that moment, fight or flight chemicals rush into your body! Now, these chemicals, or hormones, do lots of great things, here's two important ones.

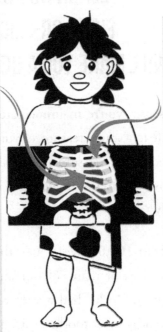

POWER SURGE!

These chemicals speed up your heart, fast! This instantly pushes blood into the muscles of your arms and legs... giving them a surge of extra power!

INCREASES FLOW OF OXYGEN!

At the same time, these chemicals cause you to hyperventilate! And this gives you more oxygen to react and move quickly!

With this extra surge of power in your body, you're able to battle those predators! Or, if you choose not to go to battle, you use your extra burst of speed... and run away from the beast. Really fast!

Fight or Flight Chemicals Can Make You a Better Athlete?

Soon, we'll teach you some cool ways to elevate your game just by using these amazing chemicals!

The chemicals our brain sends our body that
helped save Cousin Rocko, AND can help
make you a better athlete are often called:

_____ or _____

Chemicals.

Fundamental #3

YOUNG PEOPLE LEARN MINDSET TRAINING QUICKLY!

Mindset training is going to be easy for you! Let me explain why.

Let's pretend your subconscious, or the inner part of your mind, is like your bedroom. And your subconscious bedroom has a window that, when open, lets new thoughts or ideas from the outside come in.

**Young Kids'
Subconscious Window**

When you were a little kid, believing in fairies and dragons, you didn't have many thoughts and ideas yet, so your bedroom had lots of open space. Because of that, your window stayed wide open, letting new thoughts, ideas, and information come inside.

As we get older, though, our window begins to close. We become more skeptical, more rational... less open.

The subconscious bedrooms of most older adults are already filled with lots of information. Which means, most adults aren't interested in finding space to add new thoughts. So, they keep their windows shut.

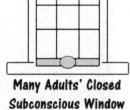

**Many Adults' Closed
Subconscious Window**

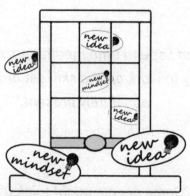

**Teens & Young Adults'
Subconscious Window**

You guys, on the other hand, probably don't mind if your bedroom's a little cluttered. You're curious and you like new things! You'll always make space for new electronics, clothes, shoes... or ideas. So, young adults tend to keep their windows cracked open a bit!

Because of how our minds work, young adults are hard-wired and more open to letting new ideas come inside.

This makes mindset training easier for you... because this type of knowledge flows more freely into your subconscious.

"I have a calmness and a poise that comes from starting the day off with meditation."

KOBE BRYANT (BASKETBALL)

"When I spend time meditating, I actually try to work on the skill set of being absolutely present."

PAUL RABIL (LACROSSE)

"Some people might think using meditation and having a mental performance side might soften you up, but it's just the opposite. It allows you to experience yourself the way you'd like to be."

DAN QUINN (FOOTBALL)

DO THIS

Write or doodle a picture to describe why you'll learn Mindset Training quicker and easier than older adults?

Fundamental #4

YOUR HIDDEN SUPERPOWER: ALPHA BRAIN WAVES

Your brain is extraordinary! It has about 86 billion nerve cells, and there's always electrical activity going on inside. And depending on what you're doing, different brain waves dominate. The main ones are your deep sleep Delta, your dreaming sleep Theta, and your awake state Beta waves.

But for upping your game, your confidence, and your happiness... **your Alpha waves are your golden ticket!**

They can do so much, like **help you stay focused, react quicker, manage stress, enter a flow state, recall information, and recover faster.**

Alpha brain waves sit between Theta and Beta. They're most active when your mind is calm and relaxed, but you're still awake.

Alpha is most active when you're daydreaming or just chilling out, not thinking too hard about anything.

You're typically in Alpha when you wake up on your own in the morning,

or when you're about ready to fall asleep.

When you feel like you're playing in the zone, where everything you do seems to be happening automatically... you're most likely playing in an Alpha state.

In Alpha, you're alert enough to give yourself direction, but relaxed enough to nudge your thinking mind out of the way.

✔ Learning how to "get into Alpha" is one of the most important mindset skills you'll learn. Let's do it now!

IMPORTANT: THIS IS HOW I'LL LEARN TO GET INTO ALPHA

The expert and pioneer in this field was a man named, José Silva. We'll use his proven countdown method to **get into Alpha.**

On the mornings you need to get up with an alarm, set two alarms. Set one for the time you need to get up and set a second alarm for 15 minutes earlier.

When your "15 minutes earlier" alarm goes off, or you wake up on your own, go to the bathroom if you need to, then come back to bed and begin your countdown to **get into Alpha.**

1. Close your eyes, and look up slightly (behind your eyelids) at about 20 degrees. For reasons not fully understood, this position of your eyes alone will trigger your brain to produce Alpha waves.

2. Begin your countdown with the number *50. Imagine you <u>SEE</u> the number in your mind, and then <u>SAY IT</u> in your mind.

3. Keep counting down, from the number 50 to 1. Each number should be "seen" and "spoken" in your mind and held there for 1-2 seconds.

4. When you reach the number 1, you will be in an Alpha state.

Do this countdown exercise again at night, shortly before you fall asleep (without alarms).

Repeat the *50 to 1 countdown for several days, and then move it to 25 to 1, then 10 to 1, and lastly, 3 to 1.

* Young people's brains naturally operate closer to Alpha, so older adults who don't meditate, may need to start with #100 and begin moving down gradually after a week at each level.

DO THIS WHEN YOU WANT TO COME OUT OF ALPHA WIDE AWAKE! (DURING THE DAY)

If you're using the countdown method to go into Alpha (other than when you're going to sleep), you may wish to come out of Alpha refreshed and wide awake. After you've reached Alpha, and you're ready to come out, slowly say these words in your mind:

1. I will slowly come out — as I count from one to five — wide awake and better than before!

2. One — two — three — four — five —

3. Eyes open! Wide awake! Feeling better than before!

✓ Practice your Alpha countdown a third time in the middle of the day.

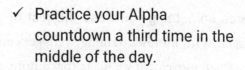
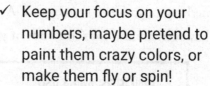

✓ Keep your focus on your numbers, maybe pretend to paint them crazy colors, or make them fly or spin!

✓ If another thought tries to sneak in during your countdown, just imagine you swipe the thought away, like you swipe on your phone.

✓ If you listen to music during this exercise, listen to music without lyrics.

✓ Better yet, listen to Alpha binaural beats during your countdown. You'll need to use headphones or earbuds for this to work. Search online for *"free Alpha binaural beats"* videos or audio recordings.

IMPORTANT: USE "FINGERS" TO TRIGGER ALPHA & EASILY GET INFORMATION INTO AND OUT OF YOUR BRAIN

Here's something you'll use the rest of your life! It's a mental trigger. With mindset training, a trigger could be a word, a breath, or a small movement we make that automatically tells our brain to do something or to feel a certain way. And the trigger you'll learn today has been around for thousands of years, because it works.

FINGERS helps you "record" information and get it into the memory and habit part of your brain.

It also helps you "hear" the answers you're looking for.

This trigger is like a shortcut. It asks our brain to please open our window, and keep it open, anytime we want to put information in... or take information out, of our subconscious bedroom.

1. You can use either hand, but you'll usually **use your non-dominant hand**, left if you're right-handed, and right if you're left-handed.

2. **Let's start by making a fist and squeeze it.** Look at your fist and notice how it's shut tight, like many people's subconscious bedroom windows.

3. Now, **relax your fist and touch the top of your thumb to the tip of the finger next to it** (your pointer finger). Some people use the two fingers next to their thumb, instead of just one finger. It works either way. Your choice. Do what feels more natural and comfortable to you.

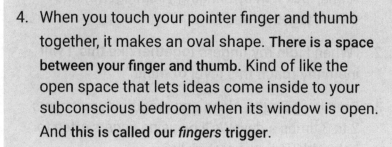

4. When you touch your pointer finger and thumb together, it makes an oval shape. **There is a space between your finger and thumb.** Kind of like the open space that lets ideas come inside to your subconscious bedroom when its window is open. And **this is called our *fingers* trigger.**

Use *fingers* when learning a new mindset tool or listening to a lecture by your teacher. Remember, *fingers* is a cue to keep your subconscious window open to absorb new ideas and information.

The cool thing is, when **you use *fingers***, it helps information go into the subconscious part of your brain where your long-term memory and habits are. **Make sure to use *fingers* a lot!**

Use *fingers* to **instantly focus and quiet all distractions during your sport,** like when shooting a free throw or hitting a ball. Or use it to **recall an answer from your memory while taking an exam.**

First, **we need to program *fingers* into your subconscious.** Like a shortcut on your computer, it needs to be programmed to know that when you click Ctrl+C or Cmd+C, that means to COPY. We need to let our brain know that when we use *fingers*, we want to open our subconscious window to achieve a specific goal or result.

THIS IS HOW YOU'LL PROGRAM "FINGERS" INTO YOUR BRAIN!

1. When doing your countdown and you've reached Alpha, **lock it in** by bringing your finger(s) and thumb together and say:

2. **"When I join my fingers together like this, I will instantly reach this level of mind."**

3. Practice going to Alpha and programming *fingers* 2 to 3 times a day! We'll be using *fingers* often to help with your mindset skills!

- ☐ Practiced Getting into Alpha ✔
- ☐ Practiced Coming Out of Alpha
- ☐ Programmed *"fingers"* into my Brain

Notes to self:

"When I train, one of the things I concentrate on is creating a mental picture of how best to deliver the ball to a teammate, preferably leaving him alone in front of the rival goalkeeper.

So, what I do, always before a game, always, every night and every day, is try and think up things, imagine plays, which no one else will have thought of, and to do, always bearing in mind the particular strength of each teammate to whom I am passing the ball.

When I construct those plays in my mind, I take into account whether one teammate likes to receive the ball at his feet, or ahead of him; if he is good with his head, and how he prefers to head the ball, if he is stronger on his right or his left foot. "That is my job. That is what I do. I imagine the game."

RONALDINHO (SOCCER)

Fundamental #5

IT'S CRAZY, BUT TRUE - PARENTS AND COACHES REALLY ARE FROM PLANET EARTH

Have you ever taken a test or quiz with a question on it that you didn't know the answer to? And it wasn't because you didn't study or memorize the answer. It was the fact that you were never taught the answer. It wasn't even in the material you were told to read.

Well, let's say that when answering the question, you guessed wrong. And you were penalized because you guessed wrong. It may have brought your grade down from an 'A' to a 'B,' all because you didn't know how to answer a question or solve a problem that you had no experience with. Is that fair?

When you were a little kid, you might have thought your parents and coaches must have a book called "How to be the Perfect Parent or Coach." How else could they know all that stuff, right?

But as you got older, you start questioning things they do - that don't seem right. **We expect our parents and coaches to do better. To be better. They're older, more experienced. They should have all the answers. The thing is... they don't.**

23

Our parents and coaches are human beings... *from planet earth*.

They were NEVER given a "how-to" manual with all the answers. They were never taught how to deal with every kind of kid, and every possible situation. Just like us, our parents and coaches don't always get it right.

And, most of the time... it's not their fault.

Parents and coaches, more often than not, just wing it, the same way you do. This human being thing... is messy. For us all.

But here's what's awesome. **When we choose to give the people in our lives a break, since we're all winging it... something inside of us happens. Something truly amazing.**

When we let go of blaming others and being mad at our parents, coaches, and teachers... it opens us up to new possibilities. It's almost as if **by choosing to recognize that we're all messed up human beings, it gives us the courage to just go for it!**

Because, really, since we're all winging it...
what have we got to lose?

CAUTION
We're All A
WORK
IN PROGRESS

Life is messy. We're messy.
Parents, coaches, me, you.
None of us do the right thing... every time.
We're all a work in progress.

Notes to self:

"It's very hard in the beginning to understand that the whole idea is not to beat the other runners.
Eventually you learn that the competition is against the little voice inside you that wants you to quit."

DR. GEORGE SHEEHAN (CROSS COUNTRY)

"Think? How are you supposed to think and hit at the same time?"

YOGI BERRA (BASEBALL)

"If you're not making mistakes, you're not doing anything!"

JOHN WOODEN
(BASKETBALL)

Fundamental #6

WHEN PART OF YOU WANTS THIS & PART OF YOU WANTS THAT – IT'S TIME TO MEET YOUR PARTS!

Do you ever say things like this to yourself? *Part of me wants to do this, but part of me doesn't! Catch the ball! Don't miss! Follow through! Focus!*

Do you ever hear your parents or coaches say things like *Get out of your head, and you'll do great! You just need to get out of your own way!*

Do you ever rip on yourself, or know someone who does, saying things like *Quit being so stupid! What's wrong with you? You're such an idiot, can't you do anything right?*

What do you think's going on?

Who's telling who... what to do?

Is our head separate from our self?

How do we get out of our OWN way?

And, who's calling who... an idiot?

Let's say you're playing your sport. In basketball, for example, pretend you're moving down the court with the ball. Part of you says, *I know I can get through those defenders and score.* Another part of you says, *No, I should play it safe, and pass the ball.*

Who are those two parts of you?

A CRUISE TO GREENLAND TO MEET MY PARTS!

If you're ready and willing... buckle up. We're about to go on an amazing adventure! It's time for you to meet your parts!

Let's use your imagination! Pretend that you've just won an all-expense paid cruise from New York to Greenland. You're going in August, but you packed sweatshirts since Greenland's chilly. Don't let its name fool you! Greenland, almost the opposite of Iceland, is not all green. In fact, it's mostly covered in ice.

When you start getting close to your final destination, imagine you're standing outside on the deck of the ship.

As your ship sails into a snowy fjord, you see something off in the distance. Movement. Others on the ship see it too.

One of Greenland's 3,000 humpback whales is breaching, jumping high over the dark polar sea. Once you get closer, this friendly, 66,000-pound swimmer, welcomes you to his summer home. An ambassador of sorts, he gives you and your fellow cruisers a little show.

When your opening act swims away, I want you to pretend that something else catches your eye. You were so captivated with your greeting whale's performance, that you didn't even notice it. Off in the distance, there it is.

A massive iceberg.

The Captain skillfully navigates his 1,000-foot-long vessel closer. The iceberg's magnificence can't be captured on film.

After taking some pictures, you put your phone down and try to take it all in. Whoever coined Disneyland® The Most Magical Place on Earth, had never sailed to Greenland and witnessed what's in front of you now.

Its white grandeur rises over 200 feet above the surface of the sea, higher than Cinderella's Castle. And, it's as long as the ship you're sailing on. You learn from the cruise director that each iceberg is a unique work of nature, no two are ever the same.

Awe-inspiring. Astounding. Amazing. It's spectacular.

And... it's a lot like our brain.

YOU'RE GOING TO MEET ONE OF YOUR PARTS – "THINKER!"

Imagine this giant iceberg, is your conscious, or **your Thinking Mind.** And let's give it a name. **We'll call it Thinker!**

Lots of things happen inside of Thinker.

Your Brain / Mind

Willpower

Thinker

Thinker is in charge of your WILLPOWER, when you need that extra determination, or force, while trying really hard to do something.

And even though willpower can be powerful, it doesn't last very long. After a little while, willpower needs time to recover, before it's ready to help you try again.

Using willpower is kind of like driving a classic muscle car as fast as you can, with the pedal to the metal. It's loud and it's forceful. But it doesn't take long before you run out of fuel.

This means you'll need to head to the gas station and fill the willpower tank back up. And, unfortunately, with willpower, the gas pump is painfully slow, and it usually takes a while before you're ready to race again.

That's why it sometimes feels like you're running out of gas when you try really hard to do something.

But it's okay! **Soon you'll learn how to use other parts of your brain that work better and faster than willpower.**

And most importantly, with these new tools, you won't feel tired because you've run out of willpower gas.

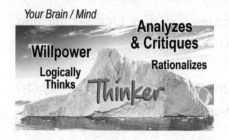

Aside from giving you willpower, **Thinker analyzes and critiques, logically thinks, and rationalizes things for you throughout the day.**

Here's an example.

Let's say in a couple of days, your team's going to play an all-star team with huge, athletic players who always seem to win.

Since that all-star team has another game the day before your game with them, your coach has Thinker go scout the team and then give you all a report.

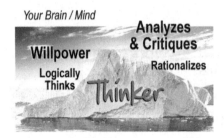

Your Brain / Mind

Analyzes & Critiques

Willpower

Rationalizes

Logically Thinks

Thinker

While carefully watching the players, Thinker, your Thinking Mind, **analyzes and critiques** the team by checking out their size, speed, skills and other things to figure out the best strategies your team should use against them.

After scouting and analyzing the team, Thinker comes to the conclusion that, no matter what your team does, **logically-thinking**, there's no way your team will win.

Well, the next day, **your team must've ignored Thinker's negative talk, because, surprise... your team does win!**

Now, one thing I didn't mention about Thinker is, **Thinker hates to be wrong.** Hates it so much, that Thinker **rationalizes** the win.

Thinker searches for excuses as to why your team won. Because, after critiquing and analyzing the data, Thinker was sure you were going to lose.

So, **Thinker comes up with rationalizations**, saying the other team must have been tired from playing yesterday, that's why they lost.

Two more Thinker things.

**Thinker loves to be in the spotlight, the
center of attention. And, Thinker talks
non-stop and *really fast*.**

Thinker's constantly thinking and talking and analyzing and
critiquing and rationalizing... over and over, all day long.

With that non-stop activity going on in your brain,
it seems like Thinker, your Thinking Mind,
is making all your decisions
and controlling everything you do and feel.

But, as the saying goes,

You can't always see the forest for the trees.
Especially when we're focused only on...
the tip of the iceberg.

IT'S TIME TO MEET THE ACTION PART OF YOUR BRAIN, "DO-IT!"

SOMETIMES
WE NEED TO
STEP BACK
TO GAIN
A LITTLE
PERSPECTIVE

And when we step back, we notice a HUGE part of the iceberg, a HUGE part of our brain... that we didn't even see.

We only noticed the tip of the iceberg, because we were too preoccupied with Thinker's non-stop noise and commotion in our head to hear or see anything else.

So now, as we step back, it becomes clear. **Less than 10% of your brain makes up your Thinking Mind.**

The rest is part of your subconscious, the Action part of your mind.

We'll call this part Do-It! Let's find out what Do-It does in this HUGE part of your brain!

Do-It's in charge of controlling your body. As a matter of fact, **Do-It's #1 job is to do whatever is necessary to keep you alive and preferably, pain free.**

And here's the interesting thing about pain.

Remember how you learned that your your brain doesn't know the difference between what's real and what you imagine?

Well, guess what? Your brain acts the same way with pain!

Emotional Pain = Physical Pain

Whether you're emotionally hurt or physically hurt, your brain sends physical sensations to your body to let you know something's wrong.

The way Do-It sees it, **pain is pain!**

When you're sad or feeling excluded, the physical pain you're feeling... is real.

Soon, you'll learn some techniques to help with all pain - emotional and physical!

LET'S LOOK AT

ALL THE THINGS "DO-IT" DOES!

✓ **Do-It Controls Your Body - muscles, organs, & cells.**

This means that Do-It can help you Improve your Muscle Memory, Performance, Speed, Reaction Time, Strength, Health, and even help you Recover From Injuries Faster!

✓ **Do-It's In Charge of Learned Behaviors & Habits.**

This means you can ask Do-It for help with Getting Rid of Bad habits or Behaviors, and Replacing Them With Good Ones, Automatically!

✓ **Do-It Stores & Helps Access Permanent Memories.**

This means Do-It can help you Find the Answers You're Looking For to Help With School, Game Plays, & More!

✓ **Do-It Loves to be Creative.**

Use Do-It to help with Art, Music, Writing, or even Figuring Out Radical Ways to Win While Gaming! Also, Do-It Can Give You Fresh Ideas to Fix Challenges at School, Home, with Sports, or Your Friends!

✓ **Do-it Controls Your Emotions**. Would you like to feel...

Courageous - *not afraid?*

Happy - *not sad?*

Relaxed - *not anxious?*

Confident - *not hesitant?*

Loved - *not alone?*

Your Brain / Mind

Analyzes & Critiques

Willpower

Rationalizes

Logically Thinks

Thinker

Do-It

Controls Our Body
-Keeps us Alive & Pain Free-

Helps us Be Creative & Think Outside the Box

Stores our Permanent Memories

In Charge of our Learned Behaviors & Habits

Controls Our Emotions

When Do-It receives a message to do something, Do-it does it. No questions asked.

Whenever you want Do-It's help, all you need to do is get the message to Do-It, and then Do-It will... do it!

But, what if Do-It's not doing what you ask? Here's a question my team and I get a lot:

> *"Sometimes I tell my brain what I want,*
> *but it doesn't always do it.*
> *So, why won't Do-It just listen to me... and do what I ask?"*
>
> (Answer: Read Fundamental #7)

List 5 things that Thinker does:

1.

2.

3.

4.

5.

List 5 things that Do-It does:

1.

2.

3.

4.

5.

Notes to self:

*"If you talk to a man
in a language he understands,
that goes to his head.
If you talk to him in his own language,
that goes to his Heart."*

NELSON MANDELA

Former President of South Africa

and Nobel Peace Laureate

Fundamental #7

DISTRACTIONS & USING THE WRONG LANGUAGE MAKE IT HARD FOR DO-IT TO HEAR YOU!

During our first few years of life, we aren't old enough to analyze or critique things, so we don't need Thinker. Besides, Thinker's not fully online in our brain yet.

Instead, the brains of little kids are like sponges. As you know, their windows stay wide open, so lots of new thoughts, ideas, and information flow easily into their subconscious bedrooms... where Do-It lives!

It's like we have a virtual reality camera that not only records things we see and experience in 3D, but it also records how things taste, smell, and physically feel. It even records how things make us feel emotionally. These recordings become memories or data, and they go straight into Do-It.

When you were a little squirt, Do-It did almost anything you asked. *"Do-It, make me a knight in shining armor driving a race car!"* And there you went, slaying sea serpents, while driving the fastest wheels on the block. Just you and Do-It, living in castles and saving the kingdom.

41

Do-It has always been a part of your life. But, Thinker didn't really become active in your brain until you stopped believing in fairies and fire breathing dragons. It happened gradually, though.

When you were little, Do-It listened to you, and did what you wanted. But, later, as you got a bit older, Thinker came online… and things started to change.

Little by little, Thinker encouraged you to be more skeptical, more critical, and to begin using analytical and reasoning skills.

As we know, Thinker's an attention-seeking, chatty know-it-all. Thinker can be helpful, but can also be very critical, and even rude from time to time.

But, like a younger sibling, no matter how annoying Thinker is, Do-It and Thinker love each other completely.

The challenge is, now that you're older,
it seeems harder for Do-It
to hear what you want because
Thinker's making so much noise.
Plus, other distractions get in the way.

DO-IT, WHY WON'T YOU LISTEN TO ME?!?

Understanding how noise in your head and other distractions affect your performance was expressed perfectly by an amazing author and tennis coach, Timothy Gallwey. He created a simple formula.

Performance = potential - interference

PERFORMANCE = POTENTIAL - INTERFERENCE. In other words, it's an easy method to figure out how you're going to perform. First, you start with your potential to do something.

For instance, pretend you're in an empty gym, field, track, or pool. You have no pressure on you at all. What's the chance you could ace that performance if there's nothing going on to annoy you, or stress you out? That would be your potential.

Then, you subtract the interference. The interference would be the noise and other distractions that are trying to get in your way.

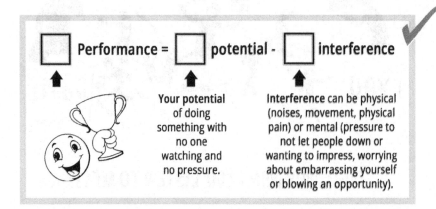

Performance = potential - interference

Your potential of doing something with no one watching and no pressure.

Interference can be physical (noises, movement, physical pain) or mental (pressure to not let people down or wanting to impress, worrying about embarrassing yourself or blowing an opportunity).

Interference could be a bunch of noise or people moving around. Or it could be the pressure or stress you're feeling. Whatever it is that's trying to get in your head and mess with your performance... that's what we call the interference.

Imagine you're good at shooting basketball free throws. Your **POTENTIAL** in making your shots is high. We'll give it a 9.

Now, let's say that Thinker is being super annoying, putting lots of negative thoughts in your head. Plus, you're stressed out about other things. So we'll give **INTERFERENCE** a 6.

Nine minus six, means your **PERFORMANCE** would only be a three, since 9-6=3. Not good.

Well, what if we could get Thinker to put a sock in it, and move some of those other distractions out of the way? What if we could bring the interference down from a 6 to a 2? Or to a 1? Or even, a 0?

Soon we'll go over some easy Mindset tools to help quiet Thinker and lessen the outside interference. But, first, there's one more important thing you need to learn.

> **The language we typically speak,**
>
> **is not Do-It's native language.**

When we use our words, Do-It has an idea of what you're saying... sort of.

Do-It understands basic requests and simple messages. But, when you try to get a more complex message or idea to Do-It *using only your words*, most of your message sounds like gibberish to Do-It.

It's like talking to foreign exchange students whose native language is not ours. The students understand some of what we say. But we can see the struggle in their eyes when we say certain phrases. It's the same with Do-It.

IMPORTANT

> To make sure that Do-It fully understands what we want,
> it's always best to use Do-It's native language,
>
> ## IMAGERY!
>
> And you already know it! You've used IMAGERY every time
> I asked you to imagine or pretend! When you used your
> senses to pretend to see, feel, hear, smell and possibly
> taste things... you created an imagined experience.
>
> ## And, that's IMAGERY!

Notes to self:

what are mindset hacks?

Think of a mindset as the way your brain interprets and responds to situations. For instance, let's say during a game you have a chance to take a shot. But, your brain thinks it's risky, and it would be embarrassing if you miss. If this happened, your brain's response might be to NOT take the shot.

Mindset "hacks" are tools or techniques that many pro and Olympic athletes use to change certain mindsets. The tools will help you build confidence, perform better, and smile more!

*"We taped a lot of famous pictures on
the locker-room doors, Bobby Orr,
Felix Potvin, John Beliveau,
all holding the Stanley Cup.*

*We'd stand back and look at them and
envision ourselves doing it.*

*I really believe if you visualize yourself doing
something, you can make that image come true.*

...I must have rehearsed it 10,000 times."

WAYNE GRETZKY (HOCKEY)

WHAT DO YOU WANT?

Mindset Hack #1

FROM NOW ON, YOU'LL TELL DO-IT <u>WHAT YOU WANT</u> - INSTEAD OF WHAT YOU "DON'T" WANT!

When we talk to Do-It, we need to remove all "not" words, including *don't, aren't, can't, cannot, couldn't, didn't, hasn't, haven't, isn't, shouldn't, wasn't, weren't, won't, wouldn't*, or anything similar. This is important because:

Do-It doesn't understand words like *'not'* and *'don't.'*

Our action brain doesn't process *not* words, especially the word *don't*. Instead, it hears and processes what you say *after* the word *don't*.

For example, sometimes kids are leaving the house and their mom yells, "*Don't slam the door!*" but they do. It's not like they try to slam it… it just happens. Or if they're ready to make a shot, and they say to themself "*Don't miss!*" but they do.

Since Do-It only hears and processes the words they hear after the word DON'T… Do-It hears, "*Slam the door!*" or "*Miss!*"

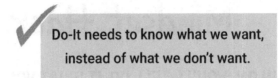

Do-It needs to know what we want, instead of what we don't want.

Let's say we want to ask Do-It for help with getting to bed earlier.

In the past, you might have said to yourself, "***Don't*** *stay up all night!*"

Now, you'll say something like, **"Do-It, please help me set an alarm for 10pm to turn off my shows & get a good night's sleep."**

Here's an idea to help you not procrastinate doing your homework.

In the past, you might have said to yourself, "***Don't*** *procrastinate doing my homework today!*"

Now you'll say something like, **"Do-It, when I get home from practice, please help me sit down at the table, and get my homework done right away!"**

And the great thing about Do-It helping you with your habits is, it only takes a little bit of effort on your part. And then, something magical happens!

Once you get the message inside of Do-It, the good habit starts to happen on its own, automatically! You won't even need to think about it!

Write down a few "not" or "don't" phrases that you sometimes say to yourself. Then next to them, write a better phrase telling Do-It what you want!

"I do creative visualization techniques in the morning. It's only 15 minutes. I used to do hours and hours of it, but I found that 15 minutes has really helped me, and it's not time-consuming at all.

"I pictured myself on the court, playing tennis, having the same feelings, feeling the shots. All of that.

There are studies that show imagery works just as well, if you do it correctly, as you actually being on the court. That's huge!"

BIANCA ANDREESCU (TENNIS)

USE IMAGERY TO CREATE A VIRTUAL REALITY EXPERIENCE IN YOUR MIND FOR DO-IT TO REALLY KNOW WHAT YOU WANT!

Mindset Hack #2

HELP DO-IT BETTER UNDERSTAND WHAT YOU WANT! USE YOUR IMAGINATION & YOUR SENSES TO CREATE A VIRTUAL REALITY EXPERIENCE!

We've already learned that Do-It's native language isn't the same as ours. If we use our "words" to ask Do-It to do something simple, like, *close the door,* Do-It understands.

But, for complex messages or ones with emotions attached, it's best to use Do-It's native language, IMAGERY.

One of the easiest ways for Do-It to help you to achieve success, no matter what you'll be doing, is to "lock in" the EMOTIONS you felt after a past success.

Here's why! Let's say you play baseball. Last year on June 17th, you were pitched a fastball, and you hit it perfectly. Seriously, the way the bat felt in your hands as it connected with the ball told you everything you needed to know. It moved with a force and velocity far surpassing any hits from your past.

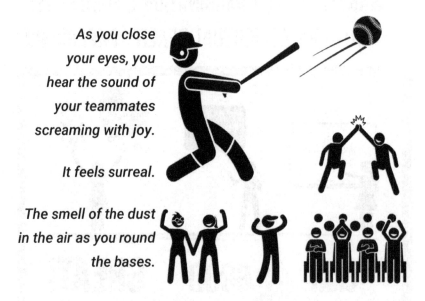

As you close your eyes, you hear the sound of your teammates screaming with joy.

It feels surreal.

The smell of the dust in the air as you round the bases.

Even the taste of victory, as a salty bead of sweat drips down to kiss your lips.

Let's pretend that today, you reach Alpha, and you tell Do-It to help you hit the ball exactly the same way you did last June 17th.

But, here's the problem. Today, instead of a fast ball, you're pitched a curve ball. Also, you've grown since June 17th. Your muscles have gotten stronger and you're an inch taller. So, asking Do-It to help you hit the ball *exactly the same way* as you hit it during your past success, *will not* give you the same triumphant result.

Instead, use IMAGERY and ask Do-It to *help you FEEL* the way you felt during and after a past success!

When you do it this way, you're trusting Do-It to make the necessary adjustments (*in your swing*) to help you once again experience the incredible feelings you felt from your past success!

This takes practice, and IT WORKS! So, keep practicing! And most importantly, *trust Do-It!*

1. Let's practice! Use *fingers* to go to Alpha.

2. Take a deep breath and say out loud, "Do-It, please help me (*hit the ball) in a way that makes me *feel* like this..."

3. Now, in your mind, recreate the emotional experience you felt after a successful past performance using imagery and your senses. Notice what you heard, saw, smelled, (maybe tasted), and physically felt from a past success you had. Make it a virtual reality experience!

4. Next, and *this is important*, take a deep breath, and inhale all the amazing emotions you felt *during* and *right after* your past success. The pride. The joy. The satisfaction. The relief.

5. Take a moment to bask in the warmth of these feelings. And then say again, "Do-It, please help me (*hit the ball) in a way that makes me *feel* like this..."

* insert whatever you want help with: sports, school, friends, pain, etc.

Describe a time you felt really good about something you did. Maybe it was in sports, in school, or maybe you did or said something that made someone else (& you) feel really good. What happened?

What did you see around you?

What sounds or voices did you hear?

How did the air feel on your skin?

Did you notice any smells or tastes?

How did your body feel?

Mindset Hack #3

WANT TO INCREASE YOUR CONFIDENCE, HAPPINESS, & PERFORMANCE? IT'S EASY BY REPLACING NEGATIVE SELF-TALK!

Research proves that switching out negative and victim self-talk phrases for "good" ones, will increase your CHP - Confidence, Happiness, and Performance!

Since Do-It's in **Do-It**  charge of your emotions and body, this means **Do-It controls your CHP!**

And, when we rip on ourselves, *it's Thinker who's talking,* because Thinker's responsible for analyzing and critiquing,

Thinker ⬇

Victim self-talk is when we don't take responsibility for something that happened. Instead we blame others. Thinker uses victim self-talk to rationalize. Thinker might say things like, *"I was on the bench because my coach is a jerk!"*

Victim self-talk is really bad because it sends a message to Do-It that the situation is out of Do-It's control. So Do-It shouldn't waste their time trying to help (*even though Do-It can help!*)

Even when we think we're being funny or humble, negative self-talk can weaken our CHP. (Like the time you mess up in your sport, tap your chest and say, "My bad!")

No matter what, always practice using "good" self-talk, and swipe away any negative self-talk that Thinker tries to send your way!

Replace Negative Phrases with These "Good" Ones!

My bad ⇨ **That's on me!**

I suck at... ⇨ **I'm getting better at...**

I'm so stupid ⇨ **I'm getting there!**

I can't... ⇨ **I'm giving it a shot!**

This is too hard ⇨ **I've got this!**

I hate when I... ⇨ **I'm getting better at...**

I wish I could... ⇨ **I'm going to...**

There's no way... ⇨ **I love a challenge!**

Life's a struggle ⇨ **Life's an adventure!**

It's not my fault ⇨ **It's on me, I've got it!**

It's so annoying... ⇨ **It's making me stronger!**

I'm such a screw up! ⇨ **Lesson learned!**

I've got the worst luck ⇨ **Tomorrow's a new day!**

I'll never be able to... ⇨ **I'll figure it out, I always do!**

The only thing standing between
you and your goal
is the story you keep telling yourself.

PEYTON MANNING (FOOTBALL)

"Don't ask yourself what you did wrong;
ask yourself what you did right."

JOHN KESSEL (VOLLEYBALL)

DO
THIS

Write down 4 "Good" Self-Talk Phrases
you're going to start using! They can
be from this book or your own!

1.

2.

3.

4.

TALK TO YOURSELF...

  LIKE YOU TALK TO YOUR FRIENDS!

Mindset Hack #4

HOW CAN YOU RE-WIRE YOUR BRAIN TO BE HAPPIER? LISTEN TO POSITIVE AFFIRMATIONS IN ALPHA!

Let's record, and listen to, affirmations while you focus on your breath! Do this in Alpha, so your subconscious window opens, and the messages get to Do-It! (Keep your eyes open as you record them.) Use any of the affirmations below and on the next page, or create your own! Then listen to these daily while repeating them out loud! (Eyes open or closed.)

1. Set your phone to record, and go someplace quiet.

2. Hit RECORD. Use fingers... as you enter Alpha.

3. With your eyes open, inhale slowly, say the first part of the phrase. Next, exhale slowly, and say the second part.

Affirmations

(*inhale*) I can. (*exhale*) I will.

(*inhale*) I train my body. (*exhale*) I focus my mind.

(*inhale*) Every day I become stronger,
(*exhale*) and more focused.

(*inhale*) I perform well, (*exhale*) under pressure.

(*inhale*) Inhale the positive, (*exhale*) exhale the negative.

(*inhale*) I focus on good health and happiness,
                    (*exhale*) I swipe away distractions.

(*inhale*) This is my time. (*exhale*) I trust myself.

(*inhale*) Today I choose kindness, (*exhale*) in everything I do.

(*inhale*) Every day in every way, (*exhale*) I am better and better.

(*inhale*) Every day in every way,
            (*exhale*) I'm more confident in everything I do.

(*inhale*) Every day in every way,
                    (*exhale*) I'm grateful for all I have.

(*inhale*) Every day in every way,
                    (*exhale*) I do better and better in school.

(*inhale*) Every day in every way,
            (*exhale*) I'm mentally and physically healthier.

 Before Bedtime, say these!

(*inhale*) I am ready and relaxed,
                    (*exhale*) for an amazing night's sleep.

(*inhale*) Good night, Thinker.
                    (*exhale*) I'll talk to you tomorrow.

Check out our website,

TheSmilingAthlete.com

to sign up and get lots of

free new hacks and tools personally emailed to you!

Also, **please leave an honest review on Amazon**
for this book, just a line or two. It would mean the world to
me. I personally read each review, and your feedback really
makes a difference!

Coach Bain

 AMAZON REVIEW PAGE:
https://rebrand.ly/smilereview
✧✧✧✧✧

Create 2 of your own affirmations!

(inhale)

(exhale)

(inhale)

(exhale)

☐ Recorded daytime affirmations.

☐ Recorded nightime affirmations.

"...going to Australia was very, very important for me. I remember about two months before that tour, I started building the kind of mindset and started to visualize about dominating their (Australia) bowlers.

I knew that I wanted to go out there and take on these bowlers, but there is no way if I keep on struggling for runs.

Eventually I had visualized it so positively, so strongly, when I went out there, my body just followed what my mind had stored two months back."

VIRAT KOHLI (CRICKET)

Mindset Hack #5

FROM NOW ON, YOU'LL "FLICK" AND "SWIPE-AWAY" NEGATIVE & DISTRACTING THOUGHTS!

Pretend your
negative self-talk
is an annoying little bug.
And, whenever a bug-thought tries to **bug you**,
just *flick it away!*

Remember, it's only a thought. It's not you.

So, whenever you hear a negative
or annoying thought,
flick it!

It's just a thought-bug.
And now, it's a thought bug...
with a headache!

1. If a negative thought buzzes around your head...
2. Say, in your mind, "Thought bug, you're out of here!"
3. Then *FLICK IT!*

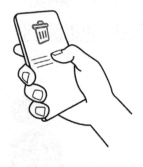

Another way to quickly get rid of distracting or negative thoughts is to pretend you're using your phone, and **SWIPE THEM AWAY!**

Do it now! Use your thumb or finger and swipe away! Physically move your thumb or finger in the air, like you do on your phone when you swipe away things you want to get rid of.

But this time, do it without your phone, while imagining negative thoughts or feelings being swiped away!

Anything you don't want there that pops in your head, swipe it away! Or use your thumb or finger to physically flick away that imaginary bug-thought!

☐ Practiced saying, "Thought bug, you're out of here!" & Flicking it!

☐ Practiced "Swiping Away" distracting or negative thoughts!

(Describing his mental rehearsal imagery sessions as)

"A sort of clarified daydream with snippets of the atmosphere from past matches included to enhance the sense of reality.

It lasts about twenty minutes and by the end of it, I feel I know what is coming.

The game will throw up many different scenarios, but I am as prepared in my own head for them as I can be."

"If you have realistically imagined situations, you feel better prepared and less fearful of the unexpected."

JONNY WILKINSON (RUGBY)

BONUS HACK: The best way to deal with Thinker, is to be proactive. When you mess up, BEFORE Thinker has a chance to butt in, use a "good" self-talk phrase to let Thinker know you've got this! Say things like:

That's on me! - I've got this!

- I'll figure it out! -

- Life's an adventure! -

- This makes me stronger! -

- Lesson learned! -

"The mind is absolutely instrumental in achieving results, even for athletes...
One of the main techniques I used was focusing on the goal and visualizing myself competing in the race before the race started...
The only one who can beat me, is me."

MICHAEL JOHNSON (TRACK)
Won 8 Olympic gold medals

"Move on to the next one.
You can't make every save or score every shot.
Have a short memory and get the next one."

JESSE
SCHWARTZMAN
(LACROSSE):

Mindset Hack #6

HOW TO STOP THOUGHTS THAT MAKE YOU FEEL BAD ABOUT YOURSELF - USE THIS EASY TOOL!

Sometimes Thinker can be a real turd. Just like a younger sibling, we might need to teach Thinker a lesson 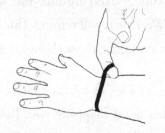  when they say stupid things. When Thinker does that, do this!

1. For 3 weeks, practice this by wearing a medium to thick rubber band on your wrist.

2. Whenever Thinker sends a negative thought to your head, *snap the rubber band!*

3. When it snaps your wrist, yell to yourself, or out loud, "Delete!"

4. And then say, "Thinker I'm good, I've got this!"

5. Optional: You can expand and explain to Thinker why Thinker is wrong, or what you're doing now to make things better.

If Thinker ever says something stupid, especially something that makes you feel bad about yourself, then snap your rubber band so it stings, just *a little!*

DELETE!

DEL

And tell Thinker, **DELETE!** Then let Thinker know that you're good and you've got this, because... you do! Regardless of what Thinker tries to put in your head!

This is also cool! Aside from it stinging a little when snapped, the rubber band is a visual cue to stop negative thoughts from coming in! Wearing the rubber band around your wrist every day is a visual cue to Thinker. Wearing it will remind Thinker that if Thinker sends you any negative thoughts, those thoughts are going to get snapped!

Plus, remember, it's Do-It's job to protect you from pain, like the pain of the rubber band snapping you. Before long, Do-It will tell Thinker to stop sending negative thoughts, so you stop feeling the pain of getting snapped by the rubber band!

EXAMPLES OF THINGS TO SAY TO THINKER AFTER SNAPPING THE RUBBER BAND

THINKER: "We lost because your defense stunk!"

"DELETE! Thinker, I'm good! I did a lot of solid things that helped my team. And even though I made a few mistakes on D, I learned what I need to do next time to play even better."

THINKER: "Don't pop out, because you always do!"

"Delete! Thinker, I've got this. You're wrong, I've only popped out three times this season, and I've learned to keep my head down for a solid hit, so that's what I'm doing!"

THINKER: "You're such a ball hog, you need to pass more."

"DELETE! Thinker, I've got this! I'm doing what coach wants me to do. And the girl who called me a ball hog was probably having a really bad day when she said that, so I'm letting it go! Thank you!"

THINKER: "You're not big enough to play in college."

"Delete! Thinker, I've got this! My mom counted 53 players bigger than me that tried out for this team who did not make it, and I did! Besides, there's plenty of players on college teams, even on pro teams, that are smaller than most of the players, and they made it! Plus, I really want this, and I work hard all the time. So, Thinker, even though your logic or statistics may say that the odds of me playing in college aren't great, I believe in myself. Heck, even Coach believes in me, so, I'm good!"

YOU'VE GOT THIS!

ATTITUDE IS MANDATORY... CAPE IS OPTIONAL!

☐   Put a rubber band on your wrist

☐   Practiced snapping it and saying "Delete Thinker!" whenever Thinker sends a negative thought to your head!

Mindset Hack #7

BE MORE CONSISTENT IN YOUR SPORT BY USING ACTION WORDS!

Some athletes have a "thing" or ritual they like to do right before they shoot, serve, or swing.

Batters will sometimes tap their shoes on the plate before hitting, wave their bat, or point to the bleachers.

Basketball players often have a ritual before they shoot a free throw. Players may lift their hand in the air without the ball and pretend to shoot, then flick their wrist to get in a rhythm.

Using Action Words, either with or without a ritual, helps you to play more consistently!

Since our goal is to get the clearest message possible to Do-It, we should use as many of our senses as possible. Combining imagery with simple Action Words can make a huge difference in your performance!

This is really important! You need to say your Action Words out loud at practice, during warmups, and in games or competitions.

Make it a habit so your Action Words come out of your mouth automatically, without even thinking about it. The reasons you want to use Action Words and say them out loud are these:

✓ It distracts Thinker from critiquing us or telling Do-It what to do. And we know that when Do-It is free from Thinker's interference, we perform our best, automatically!

✓ We're using more senses, which makes our message to Do-It even clearer! Using more senses helps Do-It have a better understanding of what we want Do-It to help us do.

✓ Plus, saying your Action Words out loud can mess with your opponents because *it switches on their Thinker*, which can cause your opponents to lose concentration!

Since you'll say your Action Words out loud during practices, your teammates will have gotten used to hearing the words, so your Action Words won't distract them.

But, when you say your action words out loud at a game or competition, *words your opponents aren't used to hearing...* you know what happens!

It *switches on* your opponent's Thinker! And when their Thinker is filling their head with thoughts like, "What in the heck is he or she talking about?" Those thoughts will distract your opponents!

Find some Action Words that "click" for you! Here's a few ideas!

BASKETBALL: While standing at the free throw line, you could use simple Action Words like, *Bounce, Bounce, Up, Swish!*

1. Physically bounce the ball and say out loud *Bounce, Bounce*.

2. Close your eyes and hold the ball in your non-shooting hand.

3. Raise only your empty shooting hand up in the air, as if you're ready to shoot, and say *Up*.

4. Flick your wrist, as if you've shot the ball and say *Swish* while using your imagination. See and hear the ball as it *swishes* through the net.

BASEBALL AND SOFTBALL: One way to get in a state of concentrated relaxation and send a clear message to Do-It would be this trick for baseball or softball.

1. Imagine your bat is a small bird.

2. Hold the bird firmly enough, so it doesn't fly away. But not so tightly that you hurt it.

3. Then, maybe say out loud,

4. *Bird, Load, Launch, Bam!*

FOOTBALL: Let's say you're an offensive lineman. And you'd like to *pancake* an opponent.

Since you'll want to use leverage and get under their pads, this might work for you.

1. While you're waiting for the snap, imagine the motion, the power and the sounds of your perfect pancake block.

2. Use all your senses to send a virtual reality image to Do-It while saying out loud,

3. *Pads, Power, Pancake!*

SOCCER/FOOTBALL: Maybe try something like this!

1. Before throwing the ball in, taking a set kick, or before sending a pass, you could - SAY OUT LOUD:

2. *Shoulders, Focus, Serve!*

3. The word Shoulders reminds you to relax your shoulders.

4. Focus keeps your attention on the target and the ball.

5. Serve tells Do-It to get the ball where you want the ball to go. Imagine it going to the back of the net or visualize it as a pass to the perfect place your teammate likes to receive the ball.

Create Action Words for your sport!

*"By focusing on the present,
[athletes] are able to quiet their mind of
pressures and anxieties and
simply focus on the play at hand."*

JULIE GARDNER (LACROSSE)

LEARNING TO USE YOUR FIGHT OR FLIGHT CHEMICALS...
HELPS YOU BRING HOME THE GOLD!

Mindset Hack #8

HOW TO INCREASE YOUR PERFORMANCE?
YOUR FIGHT OR FLIGHT CHEMICALS HELP YOU WIN!

Remember
Fundamental #2?
Learning How to Use
My Fight or Flight
Chemicals Will Make
Me a Better Athlete!

Let's dive into that - *so it will work for you!*

Do you ever watch the Olympics? I'm not sure if you've ever seen this, but there's one question that news reporters constantly ask a lot of of the Olympians, and the athletes almost always give the same answer.

REPORTER: *With thousands of people here in the arena, and over 20 million watching on television, do you ever get nervous right before your event?*

OLYMPIAN: (Most answer) *No.*

REPORTER: *But... don't you get butterflies? Sweaty palms? Doesn't your heart start to race?*

OLYMPIAN: *Of course!* (Olympians often answer.) *But those things just tell me this is important. That I'm excited! And I'm ready! Those feelings energize me! They make my body faster and stronger. They make my mind more focused. They help get me in the zone!*

And, that's the difference between most people and elite athletes. High-level performers tend to view these fight-or-flight chemicals as their partner, their friend... not their enemy. Instead of pushing those feelings away. They embrace them. They celebrate them! They give them a high-five!

They don't say, "The butterflies in my stomach feel like a bunch of bats! I can barely breathe. My heart's racing! So, this must mean, I'm going to fail!"

Instead, when they notice these things, they say to themselves:

✓ **RACING HEART**. My heart's racing! It's pumping more blood to my muscles, making me stronger and faster!

✓ **RAPID BREATHING**. I'm breathing so quickly! My lungs are sending extra oxygen to my brain, helping me be more focused and alert!

✓ **SHARPER VISION**. My pupils are dilated, letting in more light, helping me see better! Plus, my peripheral vision is elevated so I'm more aware of my surroundings and always know where my teammates and opponents are!

✓ **HEIGHTENED HEARING**. I can hear a pin drop! My senses are sharpened, I feel like a ninja!

✓ **SWEATING, COLD HANDS AND GOOSEBUMPS**. I'm sweating, my hands feel cold, and I've got goosebumps! This is perfect because it means my blood is being diverted to my brain and major muscles, arming me for combat!

✓ **NO PAIN**. Any pain or soreness I may have felt before is temporarily gone! I'm now able to focus completely on the challenge ahead!

✓ **DRY MOUTH AND NOT HUNGRY**. My mouth is dry, and I can't eat! This means my digestive system is shutting down which tells me that it's all hands-on-deck. My body's resources are mobilized for battle!

✓ **BUTTERFLIES**. The wonderful butterflies in my stomach? Those little guys remind me of just how much I want this! Motivating me to keep pushing through! At the same time, they form a protective circle around me ...always keeping me safe!

Before they're about to begin competing, most high-level performers don't ask the warriors in their stomach to calm down. Nope, it's quite the opposite. Elite athletes and high-level performers usually have a very different conversation with those fluttering soldiers.

**"Butterflies, it's time to get in formation!
We're going to battle!"**

You see, guys, it's our mindset, our attitude that makes the difference. When you *flip the switch* and understand that your chemicals are there to help you... that's when you'll bring home the gold!

Before you compete, sometimes your Fight or Flight chemicals cause these things to happen. How are they helpful?

Racing heart:

Heightened hearing:

Butterflies:

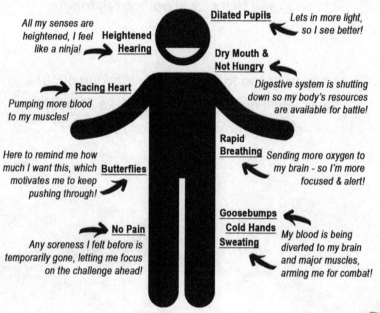

Fight or Flight Chemicals
Prepare Our Body for Competition!

IMPORTANT

Dilated Pupils — *Lets in more light, so I see better!*

All my senses are heightened, I feel like a ninja! → **Heightened Hearing**

Dry Mouth & Not Hungry — *Digestive system is shutting down so my body's resources are available for battle!*

→ **Racing Heart**
Pumping more blood to my muscles!

Here to remind me how much I want this, which **Butterflies** *motivates me to keep pushing through!*

Rapid Breathing *Sending more oxygen to my brain - so I'm more focused & alert!*

→ **No Pain**
Any soreness I felt before is temporarily gone, letting me focus on the challenge ahead!

Goosebumps Cold Hands Sweating *My blood is being diverted to my brain and major muscles, arming me for combat!*

Sweating, cold hands, & goosebumps:

Dry mouth & not hungry:

Dilated pupils:

Rapid breathing:

Sensations of pain are gone:

*"I learned a long time ago
that there is something worse than missing the
goal, and that's ...not pulling the trigger."*

MIA HAMM (SOCCER)

*"If you spend too much time thinking about a
thing, you'll never get it done. Make at least one
definite move daily toward you goal."*

BRUCE LEE (MARTIAL ARTIST)

Mindset Hack #9

HOW TO GET YOUR GRADES UP – PART 1
YOUR FIGHT OR FLIGHT CHEMICALS MAKE IT EASY!

Here's the deal with tests and exams, and this is important. Your fight or flight chemicals not only help you physically perform at a higher level... they also help you do better in school, even on exams.

✓ **ENERGY TO POWER THROUGH** - The adrenaline releases extra energy into your bloodstream, giving you strength to power through the exam!

✓ **EASIER RETRIEVAL OF ANSWERS** - Your chemicals open the door to your memory banks, making it easy to retrieve the answers you're looking for!

✓ **MORE FOCUSED AND ALERT** – These chemicals send extra oxygen to your brain, making you focused and alert. This gives your brain extra power!

✓ **INCREASED AWARENESS AND PERCEPTION** - Plus, that extra oxygen also makes your senses and intuition sharper! This helps you understand the questions on exams better and makes you more aware and clued-in when doing homework!

✓ **PROTECTION** - And those wonderful butterflies in your stomach? Your fluttering soldiers will fly out and form a circle around you, helping you feel safe and protected. This allows you to focus better on your exam, undisturbed.

✓ **ADDED MOTIVATION** - Plus, your butterflies also remind you that this test or schoolwork is important, motivating you to keep pushing though, just like with sports!

AND CHECK THIS OUT! There was an amazing research project done a little while ago by Harvard psychologist Jeremy Jamieson, and it suggests that feeling stressed does NOT hurt performance on tests. As a matter of fact, it can HELP performance!"

Research shows that *"...people who feel anxious during a test, might actually do better."*

It's true! And, as a serious athlete... you're already the kind of person who performs better under pressure, whether you know it or not. This means that instead of being worried when you feel stressed or anxious before a test, you should feel the opposite! You should be excited! Just "flip the switch" on your mindset to change your attitude! Those fight or flight chemicals are here to help you!

But, if you're like a lot of students, you might be thinking this.

"In the past, when I felt stressed out right before a test, I didn't do well. So, how exactly does "flipping the switch" on my mindset make things better?"

(Answer: Read Mindset Hack #10!)

When Fight or Flight chemicals are released before you take an exam,

How does the surge of adrenaline help?

What do your chemicals open?

Your chemicals send extra oxygen to your brain? List 2 ways this helps:

What are 2 ways your butterflies help?

The results from an amazing research project by Harvard psychologist Jeremy Jamieson shows that:

"...people who feel anxious during a test, might _____ ___ _____."

"Breathe, believe, and battle.
My former coach, Troy Tanner,
told us that before each match.
Breathe – be in the moment.
Believe – have faith that
you can rise above it.
Battle – you gotta be prepared
to go for as long as it takes."

KERRI WALSH (VOLLEYBALL)

"I start months before the event.
I just sit there and visualize the race in my
mind, I dive into the pool. I'm swimming
strongly. I'm out in front. The crowd
roaring, I can hear them. No one can catch
me. I even see myself ...with the gold
medal placed around my neck."

KIEREN PERKINS (SWIMMING):

Long Distance Swimmer, Broke 11 World Records

Sports Illustrated GREATEST
Sportsman of the 20th Century,
Olympic Gold Medalist &
3-Time Heavyweight Champion Boxer

Muhammad Ali:

"I am the Greatest!
I said that even before
I knew I was!"

Mindset Hack #10

WANT HELP WITH HOW YOU REACT TO SITUATIONS? JUST "FLIP THE SWITCH" ON YOUR MINDSET! THIS STORY HELPS YOU LEARN HOW!

As an athlete, I'm going to assume you lift weights. What I want you to do is use your imagination... and **pretend you're at the gym.** Now, imagine you notice another kid at the gym lifting weights. His name is Max. Max is about your height. But, unlike you, **Max does not look like he lifts**. At all.

But Max is lifting, almost every day, which is awesome! The problem is, Max is only using five and ten-pound dumbbells. And he's not doing many reps.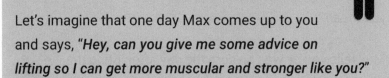

Let's imagine that one day Max comes up to you and says, *"Hey, can you give me some advice on lifting so I can get more muscular and stronger like you?"*

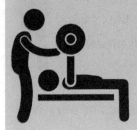 You explain to Max that in order to gain more muscle mass, he'll either need to **lift more weight or do a lot more reps.** And on that day, you show him how. You recommend a muscle-building workout.

 You spot Max and help him lift some heavier weights. You even ask a trainer at the gym to make sure that what you suggested is safe and appropriate for Max's size and build. Max is doing everything you and the trainer suggested. He's working really hard. You're impressed.

But over the next two days, Max is not at the gym. On the third day, though, Max is back. But he's also **back to lifting just a few reps with the lightweight dumbbells.**

Of course, you're confused. And to be honest, a little frustrated. You took the time to help Max, and he's totally ignoring everything you taught him.

Let's now **pretend you walk up to Max and ask how he's doing**. Max tells you he feels better now, but his body is obviously very different from yours. You're like, "*What do you mean?*'"

Max tells you he was so sore the day after lifting the heavy weights, that he thought he was going to die. He could barely move the next few days. Max said, "*My body is obviously not the kind of body meant to lift heavier weights, like yours is.*"

A GOOD SORE = A NEW MINDSET. Being the very nice

person that you are... you don't laugh at Max. Instead, you tell Max that **when we lift heavy weights, or do lots of reps using lighter weights, we cause micro-tears in our muscles. And micro-tears are what we want.**

You explain that even though there's soreness, those microscopic tears begin to repair themselves relatively quickly.

 And, as many of you know, but Max did not understand, **it's that repair to the micro-tears that gives us muscle growth.** You tell Max that we call this a *good sore* because it means our micro-tears are being repaired, and our muscles are growing!

After your explanation, Max's attitude... or Max's *mindset*, about the soreness, has changed. Max *flips the switch* on his thinking!

Micro-tears aren't bad, they're good! And because you took the time to explain this to Max, Max starts lifting heavier weights. **Max *powers through the temporary discomfort*, and soon, Max's muscles grow!**

Remember the Olympians? When the reporters asked the Olympians if they get butterflies, have sweaty palms and a racing heart before their event, what did they say? They said, "Yes."

Assuming that Max is lifting a lot more reps or heavier weights, do you believe that Max still feels sore afterwards?

So, let's break this down.

1. Max still gets sore on most days after lifting.

2. Max now understands this soreness is good, because the soreness is from micro-tears which help Max build muscle.

3. Max uses "good soreness" as a secret weapon, to reach his goal to gain more muscle!

Max flipped the switch on his mindset! Now you do it!

1. You may still get butterflies, sweaty palms and a racing heart right before a game or competition.

2. You now understand these sensations are good, because they're caused by chemicals which will help your performance.

3. You use these chemicals as your secret weapon, to win!

Awesome! Now do it again for when you're stressed in school!

1. You may still get butterflies, sweaty palms, and a racing heart right before a big test.

2. You now understand these sensations are good, because they're caused by chemicals which will help you do better.

3. You use your chemicals as your secret weapon, to improve your grades!

You've always had this secret weapon to help you perform at a higher level and get better grades.

It's just that no one ever explained to you that your fight or flight chemicals are not something to be afraid of.

Instead, these amazing fight or flight chemicals will not only save you from a saber tooth, but they can also help you do better in school and win games and competitions!

So, the next time you get butterflies, sweaty palms or feel your heart racing... are you going to push your chemicals away? Or are you going to give them a high-five?

Your brain, at positive, [like when we're happy] is 31% more productive than your brain at negative, neutral or stressed." [Research shows] "Your intelligence rises, your creativity rises, your energy levels rise."

SHAWN ACHOR
HARVARD RESEARCHER &
AUTHOR of *The Happiness Advantage* & *Big Potential*

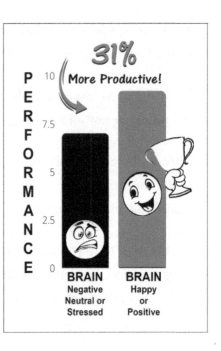

A SOFT BED? A TROPICAL BEACH?...
TRANSPORT YOURSELF TO "YOUR SPECIAL PLACE"

Mindset Hack #11

INSTANTLY FEEL HAPPY, CALM, & SAFE? THIS EASY HACK USES YOUR "FEEL GOOD" CHEMICALS!

Now it's time for some Feel Good Chemicals! As I'm sure you understand, we can't always be in a fight or flight mode. We'd be exhausted. It takes too much energy. Instead, **we need to balance our life and spend most of our time in a rest and digest mode.** This is where our body and mind feel comfortable and secure.

When we're in a place or doing an activity that we associate with feeling happy, calm, and safe, our brain releases Feel Good Chemicals.

In a minute, you'll learn how to instantly flood your bloodstream with these amazing chemicals, no matter what you're doing. You'll practice imagining yourself in *Your Special Place*, wherever that might be. You choose *Your Special Place* to be anywhere you want.

You may choose your bed. Imagine your homework is done and you're lying there listening to music or watching a show. You may notice the sensation of your cushiony mattress under your body. You might sense the softness of a sheet or comforter gently cradling your skin, making you feel *snug as a bug in a rug*.

Whatever makes you feel cozy and relaxed, protected and at peace, is what you'll feel.

95

When you're there, enjoy these safe and restful sensations. Breathe them in.

Maybe you imagine that you're on a tropical beach, as the sun melts away any tightness inside your muscles. Laying on the warm sand, hearing the pounding of the waves crashing against the shore, drowning out your thoughts.

Or you might imagine that you're just hanging out, surrounded by people you love, doing absolutely nothing. It will be your choice, the sky's the limit. This is *your special place.*

Practice the following exercise daily over several weeks. Then, whenever you want to submerge yourself in your Feel Good Chemicals, use *fingers*, and take a few deep, slow breaths. Next, imagine yourself instantly transported to *Your Special Place.*

And as you do, allow your brain to flood your bloodstream with your incredible, rest and digest, Feel Good Chemicals!

You may wish to record this into your phone and then play it back with your eyes closed. If you do, speak slowly, and pause to allow time between each number listed.

DO THIS

1. Lean back or lie down... and close your eyes.

2. *Fingers.* (touch your thumb to the finger(s) next to it, making an oval.)

3. Place one of your hands just below your ribcage, near your belly button.

4. Now, focus on your breathing. *Nice and low,* just above your belly button. *In and out,* naturally. Notice how it feels. *In... and out.* Continue to focus on each breath... *in... and out. Nice and low.*

5. Feel your hand *slowly rise up,* as you inhale. *And down,* with each exhale. *In... and out. Up... and down.* Keep focusing on each breath... you know how. *In, and out,* naturally. Notice how it feels. Breathing low, near your belly. *Up... and down.* Focus on each breath... *in... and out.*

6. Now transport yourself to *Your Special Place.* Take it all in. The colors and smells. The sounds, the air. **You're so content. You're so happy**.

7. If an outside thought starts to wander into your mind, simply *swipe that thought away...* like you do on your phone. *Swipe away.* It's no big deal. *Swipe it away.* Then return your focus to your breath, to *Your Special Place.*

8. As your hand *rises and falls* with each breath, notice how good you feel.

9. You find yourself feeling this way, *automatically,* anytime you want. Just take a moment to focus on your breathing. Then allow your imagination to transport you to *Your Special Place.*

10. It's so simple, yet few do it. But you're in a special group, because *you take a few minutes each day to train your mind.*

YOU OWN YOUR EMOTIONS...
MINDSET HACKS & TOOLS HELP YOU CONTROL THEM!

Mindset Hack #12

WANT TO KNOW A SECRET TO GET RID OF SAD OR ANNOYING EMOTIONS? THIS IS A GAME CHANGER!

1. I'd like you to set a timer on your phone for 90 seconds.

2. When you're ready, hit "START" on your timer, and do 90 seconds of burpees! Yes! 90 seconds of burpees! You've got this! I KNOW you can do it!

3. When you're done, come back to this page!

(If you're injured or cannot physically do burpees, do something else that is physically stressful and tiring for 90 seconds.)

All done? How was it? Did it suck? Probably. But, was it bearable? You obviously handled it! 90 seconds isn't that bad, right?

Now, we've talked a lot about the chemicals released from our brain. And sometimes we love the way those chemicals make us feel, physically or *emotionally*. And, then again, sometimes we don't. Let's focus on *emotional sensations* for this mindset hack.

These chemicals sent from your brain may cause you to feel certain ways, such as scared, worried, or stressed-out. These chemicals may also produce emotions that allow you to feel safe, calm, loved, or happy. There's thousands of other "feelings" you may experience.

But, there's something I haven't shared with you yet about this rush of chemicals that's very, very important. This first part you already know:

> To activate an emotion, your brain receives a thought (positive or negative), and then it sends a rush of chemicals into your bloodstream.
> Those chemicals activate certain bodily sensations, sometimes pleasant, sometimes not.

We've already learned several mindset hacks and tools to squash negative thoughts before Thinker is able to get them into your head. For the thoughts that do get in, we've also learned ways to quickly get them out of your head before your brain sends the chemicals.

Yet, sometimes, a sneaky negative thought gets inside and sticks around long enough for our brain to send a rush of chemicals that cause us to feel emotions we don't like.

But here's something **VERY IMPORTANT** that I haven't told you yet. According to neuroscientist, Dr. Jill Bolte Taylor:

> This rush of chemicals leave your bloodstream within 90 seconds. So, if we can get rid of that negative thought, it won't be around to trigger a second, or a third rush of chemicals. Which means, after 90 seconds...
> the uncomfortable feelings will go away!

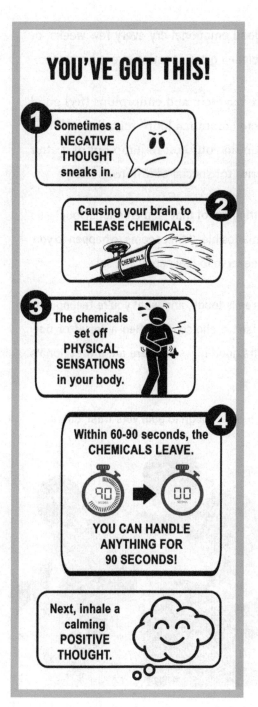

YOU'VE GOT THIS!

1 Sometimes a NEGATIVE THOUGHT sneaks in.

2 Causing your brain to RELEASE CHEMICALS.

CHEMICALS

3 The chemicals set off PHYSICAL SENSATIONS in your body.

4 Within 60-90 seconds, the CHEMICALS LEAVE.

90 SECONDS → 00 SECONDS

YOU CAN HANDLE ANYTHING FOR 90 SECONDS!

Next, inhale a calming POSITIVE THOUGHT.

Does 90 seconds sound familiar? You can handle almost anything, *even burpees*, for 90 seconds.

So, the secret to getting rid of sad or annoying emotions?

Wait 90 seconds! Then inhale a calming, positive thought! And do anything else you need to do to get that negative Thinker thought out of your head!

You've already learned some ways to do this!

Flick that thought bug! *Swipe Away* and *delete* that unwanted negative self talk! *Snap* that rubber band! Get that negative thought out of there!

It's also nice to know that a good emotional cry every few weeks, or once a month, is awesome at cleaning out negative stress hormones.

Plus, emotional tears produce oxytocin and endorphins (feel good chemicals)! So, staying in a "sad emotional loop" for a little while is totally fine. Just make sure you do your best to jump out of it after a bit... and save those good cries for special occasions.

IMPORTANT: Sometimes getting out of that "sad emotional loop" - *no matter how hard you try* - feels impossible. If that seems to happen to you, *please* let someone know. You deserve to feel happy and safe.

You're dealing with something really tough, and what you're feeling isn't your fault. Feeling depressed isn't a choice, it's often a result of how chemicals work in our brain. The good news is, there are professionals who can help with that!

And when the right counselor is lucky enough to gain your trust, they'll toss you a lifebuoy. Then after you're able to come up for air, they'll arm you with some amazing tools to help you feel a little bit better, day by day.

Remember, it's okay. **We're all... a Work In Progress.** :)

1. Find an uplifting song that helps you feel happy and light, be sure it's at least 90 seconds long.

2. Download it on your phone.

3. Whenever a rush of chemicals floods your bloodstream that causes you to feel sad or upset, immediately play your "happy" song.

4. When the song is over, the chemicals are flushed out of your bloodstream.

Understanding Sad or Annoying Emotions

Sometimes a negative thought sneaks in causing your brain to _____ _____.

The chemicals set off _____ _____ in your body. Within ____ seconds, the chemicals _____.

Next, inhale a calming _____ _____.

"When I want to turn it on, I have a routine I go through.
I get away from the plate.
I stretch, control my breathing,
and slow up my heart rate. I slow up.
I start toward the plate, and
I imagine myself putting the 'sweet spot' in the hitting
area just as the ball is getting there.
I see a line drive going to center field.
It's important to me to see myself putting that bat there
and not swinging it.
When I visualize, I feel my approach
and the contact.
I remind myself to see the release
and the spin on the ball.
Then, I 'see it' the way I'm going to see it.
I don't want to try too hard or tense up.
As I step into the batter's box, I mumble
'All right Reggie, just let it happen,
just let it flow... Now, let it happen.'
Then, I am quiet."

REGGIE JACKSON
(BASEBALL)

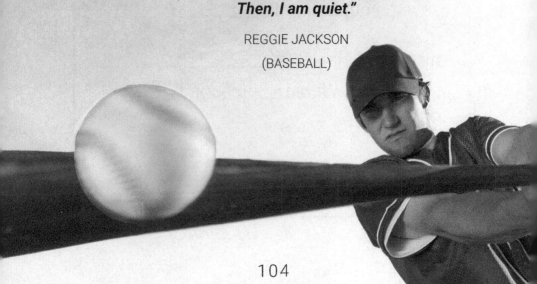

104

Mindset Hack #13

HOW TO MASTER A NEW SKILL IN HALF THE TIME? THIS DOCTOR FROM JOHN HOPKINS SHOWS US HOW!

Here's a mind-blowing technique you can use to learn a motor skill faster than you ever thought possible!

A recent study from Dr. Pablo Celnik and his team at Johns Hopkins University showed a way to master a new skill up to twice as fast as normal. It's true! You might only need to do half as many repetitions to turn your skill into a muscle memory!

1. **Spend time practicing your skill normally,** like hitting balls in a batting cage, over and over again, the same normal way.

2. **Then pause and wait a while, at least a few hours.**

3. **Later that day, add a slight change or variation. Then practice over and over again with that change.** For instance, the next time you hit, switch it up a bit. Dr. Celnik says the changes in the training need to be small, like a little adjustment to the size or weight of the bat, stick, racket, or ball. Or maybe try shooting the ball or puck from exactly the same spot in the normal session, then move it a few inches during the "slight change" session.

4. **Let your brain soak it all in overnight.**

5. **The next day, practice the normal way.**

According to Dr. Celnik's research, when we do this, we learn our skills faster than if we had practiced the normal way at each session.

Do this as often as you can. Ask your coach if you and your team can work this into practices!

Add *fingers*! Add imagery! Add some of the other amazing mindset hacks and tools you've learned!

By using mental tools during practice, like this awesome one from Dr. Celnik, you can speed up the process of learning new skills and turn your tasks into muscle memory faster and easier!

Notes to self:

"VENTURE OUTSIDE YOUR COMFORT ZONE.
THE REWARDS ARE WORTH IT." --RAPUNZEL

"IT'S UP TO YOU, HOW FAR YOU'LL GO.
IF YOU DON'T TRY, YOU'LL NEVER KNOW!" -- MERLIN

"YOU'RE BRAVER THAN YOU BELIEVE,
AND STRONGER THAN YOU SEEM,
AND SMARTER THAN YOU THINK." -- WINNIE THE POOH

"ALL IT TAKES IS FAITH AND TRUST... AND A LITTLE BIT OF PIXIE DUST."
-- PETER PAN --

SOMETIMES IT TAKES COURAGE TO DO SOMETHING KIND.
BE BRAVE. IT'S WORTH IT!

Write down 2 nice things you will do for someone by this date: _____

1.

2.

Mindset Hack #14

WANT TO FEEL LESS NERVOUS BEFORE A BIG GAME, TEST, OR TALKING TO SOMEONE YOU LIKE? JUST DO THIS!

Research studies prove that doing nice things for others actually helps us... *just by doing them!* The person doing the kind act gets a boost in serotonin, which makes them feel happier. Do something nice for someone else before a big game, test, or anything else that freaks you out! It helps you to not feel as stressed and nervous.

It even helps you feel less awkward.

Plus, the happiness boost you'll get will help improve your performance, since research shows that happy people perform better!

When You Do Something Kind for Another Person:

You'll get a boost of serotonin which makes you feel happier, less stressed out, less nervous & less awkward!

*"...focusing on your attitude
will keep you in check. I am a big believer
that everything will fall into place with the
right attitude. Jerry [Harris, from 'Cheer'"]
said it best the other day:*

*'To have an attitude for gratitude,'
meaning: be thankful for the
things you have in life,
and not to focus on the negatives."*

MONICA ALDAMA (CHEER)

Mindset Hack #15

HOW TO GET YOUR GRADES UP – PART 2
AND, SPEND LESS TIME STUDYING!
SCIENCE SHOWS US HOW WITH THIS HACK!

This hack is based on research in how our brain is wired to learn while we study. We'll call it **22 & 8**.

The first thing we do is a brain warm up. Before starting your study session, **for 2 minutes, you'll do some intense cardio.** Make sure it's fierce, hard-core cardio. Since you're an athlete, you need to take it up a notch for 2 minutes. Run or do jumping jacks, pushups, sit ups, whatever you want, as long as you go at it hard for 2 minutes.

This brain warmup is really important. There have been so many research studies and they all show the same thing. Doing high intensity exercise, for even just 2 minutes before you study or take

22&8 Study Session

BRAIN WARMUP:
2 Minutes of
Intense Cardio
(Effects last for 2 hours)

IMPORTANT:
Put Your Phone in
Airplane Mode

1. Study HARD for
22 Minutes

2. Enjoy 8 Minutes
of Free Time

3. Study HARD for
22 Minutes

4. Enjoy 8 Minutes
of Free Time

a test, improves learning memory, planning, problem solving, concentration and verbal fluency.

And what's really cool, **the brain warmup helps keep you learning better for up to two hours without having to do the cardio again!**

Then comes the **22 & 8** part! **For 22 minutes you'll study hard.** You'll stay completely focused.

This means you **put your phone in airplane mode**. The only thing you'll use your phone for is to set a timer for 22 minutes, and then 8. Seriously. If you need to do something online for studying, use a computer so you don't start looking at social media or videos or something.

Then **after you've completely focused and studied hard for 22 minutes, you have 8 minutes to do whatever you want.** Get on your phone, watch part of a movie, grab a light snack, whatever you want. The 8 minutes of free time is your reward because you were completely focused with your 22 minutes of studying.

There's a scientific reason for this. Basically, your brain does a great job of absorbing about 22 minutes' worth of information. Afterwards, it needs a few minutes to let the material soak in.

Then, **after the 8 minutes of free time, start over again with 22 minutes of intense studying.**

And it's best not to study for more than 2 hours total. After 2 hours, go eat a meal or watch a show. Give yourself at least an hour break before you start back up, if you have to.

COACHES: YOU SHOULD ALSO USE THIS SCIENCE, ESPECIALLY WHEN TEACHING NEW SKILLS OR PLAYS.

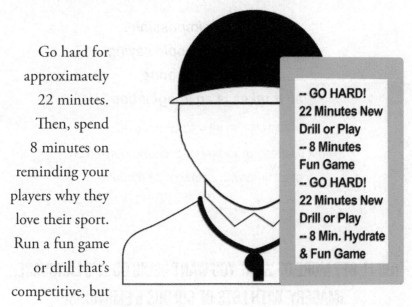

Go hard for approximately 22 minutes. Then, spend 8 minutes on reminding your players why they love their sport. Run a fun game or drill that's competitive, but requires little thought and no judgment, for 8 minutes.

-- GO HARD!
22 Minutes New Drill or Play
-- 8 Minutes Fun Game
-- GO HARD!
22 Minutes New Drill or Play
-- 8 Min. Hydrate & Fun Game

After that short break, come back to the new skill or run the new play again. After two rounds, you'll be pleasantly surprised at how well that new skill or information soaked into Do-It, the automatic part of your players' brains.

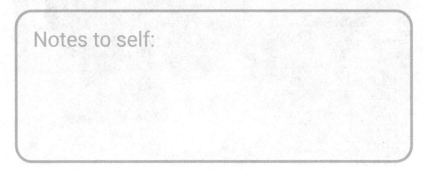

Notes to self:

*"Nothing is impossible.
With so many people saying
it couldn't be done,
all it takes is an imagination."*

MICHAEL PHELPS (SWIMMING)
Most successful and most decorated Olympian
of all time with a total of 28 medals

YOU'LL GET MORE OF WHAT YOU WANT USING DO-IT'S LANGUAGE...
IMAGERY, WITH LOTS OF COLORS & EMOTIONS!

Mindset Hack #16

HOW TO GET YOUR GRADES UP – PART 3
YOU JUST NEED TWO THINGS FOR THIS HACK!

This easy hack helps connect test questions with answers using Do-It's language of imagery (using lots of senses). And you'll only need some note cards and colored pens or markers.

You won't be using your phone or computer, since that would limit you to mainly only using your sense of sight and touch. Instead, you'll handwrite the information you're studying on notecards, using your sense of sight (with many colors), touch, and also kinesthesia, your sense of movement, by moving the markers and note cards.

Plus, studying only on electronics limits your sense of sight, since you're typically only seeing one color and one size of text.

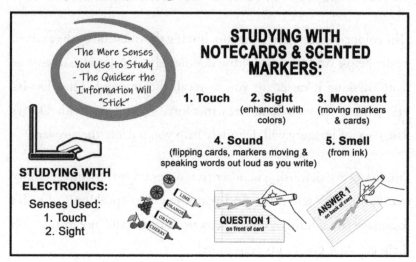

If you want to really go crazy, get some scented markers! Think grape, cherry, orange, and lime. Do-It will love it!

Remember, Do-It will be able to help you learn more and do better on tests when you speak in Do-It's language. Give Do-It a virtual reality "*show*" of what you need to learn, by using lots of senses!

Another cool tool or trick when you're studying questions and answers is to use the same color for the answer to the question you write down. For instance, write the questions on one side of the notecard and the answer on the back with the same color ink!

As an example, say you're studying for a history exam. On a card, you could use a purple, grape scented marker and write *Seeker of the fountain of youth* on one side and the answer, *Ponce de Leon* on the back. Maybe even doodle a picture of a fountain next to his name! On another card, use an orange marker and write *French heroine in the Hundred Years' War* and *Joan of Arc* in orange on the back. And maybe doodle "100" and circle it next to her name!

The color connection in the brain, linking the question to the answer, really helps! And those fun little doodles give Do-It more to engage with, making it easier for you to recall the answers! Plus, Do-It's responsible for your long-term memory, so studying with Do-It's language of imagery will definitely help you retrieve the answers!

Studies prove that using handwritten notes improves your memory recall when it's test time. And you know that speaking in Do-It's language, by adding colored pens or markers and notecards, will help get your grades up even more!

☐   Got some notecards to study with

☐   Got colored pens or markers
(maybe even scented ones!)

Notes to self:

"It's probably the biggest difference this year, my commitment to meditation and mindfulness, I feel like I've just been so much more aware of my emotions and my thoughts. I've been able to refocus, re-center, change the story."

"I'm so much more calm. I don't let the moment get away from me or something be too big or something bother me for too long. I was good at hiding it. I'm never one to vocalize things or try to show anybody my emotions, that's always been something, like, nobody should see how I'm feeling. Especially the opponent, I don't want them to know if they were getting at me, but mentally, sometimes they were."

"...you're going to have moments where there are ups and downs, but I can really stay present. It's been awesome."

ELENA DELLE DONNE
(WNBA - BASKETBALL)

Mindset Hack #17

AMAZING GAME STATS FROM RESEARCHER PROVE YOUR COACHES & PARENTS WERE RIGHT!

You always hear how getting a good night's sleep is important before games. But will it really make a difference in your performance? Here's data from sleep expert, Dr. Cheri Mah, after she worked with an NBA player and a D1 college basketball team.

4-time NBA champion, Andre Iguodala, was already a star with the Golden State Warriors when Dr. Mah entered his life. But, Andre used to always stay up super late playing video games. To help him play better, she (and he) knew he needed a better sleep routine.

Dr. Mah had Andre limit his caffeine, use a nighttime wind-down routine, and do a few other things. He used cool sheets, and didn't sleep in athletic clothing, "Because," he said, "it throws the brain off, it thinks you're ready to work out," instead of going to sleep. He avoided long naps, and in his bedroom, he put his phone in airplane mode and turned the TV off. And look what happened!

NBA: ANDRE IGUODALA - After Sleep Improvement:
- ✓ Free throw percentage went up 8.9%
- ✓ Points per minute increased by 29%
- ✓ Fouls per game went down 45%
- ✓ Turnovers per game decreased 37%

And check this out! Before working with professional athletes, Dr. Mah helped conduct a sleep research experiment with 11 players on the Stanford Men's Basketball Team.

In just two weeks of increasing their sleep to 10 hours per night, along with them not drinking coffee or alcohol, and adding daytime naps when they couldn't get in 10 hours of nighttime sleep, this is what happened. They were faster and their shooting percentage increased by big numbers.

STANFORD MEN'S BASKETBALL TEAM
After only two weeks:

✓ In 282' sprints, they decreased their times from 16.2 seconds to 15.5

✓ Free throws increased by 9%

✓ 3-point shots made increased by 9.2%

While traveling, Dr. Mah also suggested maybe wearing a sleep mask and ear plugs, and listening to white noise (there's lots of apps for your phone). Also, the blue light from your phone screens makes your brain more active. So, be sure to go into your phone's Settings and turn on the Nighttime or Night Shift setting.

Another tool is to put a small notepad and pencil by your bed. Before you go to sleep, take a minute and write down your to-do list for the next day in the notepad (avoid using your phone). And, if there's anything else on our mind, write it down in the notepad, too.

The idea is to get those *Thinker thoughts* out of your head.
That way Thinker won't keep you awake thinking about them. And since you wrote them on your to-do list, Thinker knows you'll get to them tomorrow.

And if Thinker wakes you up in the middle of the night, do this. Keep your phone and light off. Then, grab the pencil and notepad by your bed and write down the Thinker thought that's in your head.

Who cares if you're writing in the dark and the words are all over the page? No phone or lights! Just tell Thinker thanks for the thought and you'll get back to them the next day... *after* you've had a good night's sleep.

"Sleep is all about recovering. So, if you're not sleeping, you're not recovering. And if you're going to break your body down a lot, you better find ways to build it back up."

Tom Brady, NFL 7 Time SuperBowl Champion

SLEEP EXPERT, DR. CHERI MAH'S 6 TIPS FOR BETTER SLEEP

A growing list of professional teams in the NBA, NFL, NHL and MLB are turning to Dr. Mah to fine-tune their athletes' sleeping schedules. Here's what to do!

1. Athletes should get 8 to 10 hours plus of sleep every night.

2. Maintain a regular bedtime and wake-up time – *Set an alarm to go off 30 minutes before you start your wind-down routine.*

3. Implement a wind-down routine.

"A 20- to 30-minute wind-down helps you transition to sleep," Dr. Mah said. "Reading is great – a real book, not an iPad or phone that emits blue frequencies of light, which can negatively impact sleep. For athletes, I recommend stretching or yoga."

4. Make your room like a cave.

Dr. Mah said, "You want it to be really dark, quiet and cool, as well as comfortable. For darkness, I recommend blackout curtains; some people prefer eye masks. For quiet, use earbuds or earplugs. For cool, set your temperature at 60 to 67 degrees."

5. Reduce your intake of caffeine and alcohol.

"Caffeine has a half-life of about six hours, so it's best to cut out caffeine in the late afternoon and evening," Dr. Mah said. "And alcohol fragments sleep, particularly in the early morning hours."

6. Take 20 – 30 minute power naps.

"Power naps are great," Mah said. "Keep naps short....For athletes, I do recommend pre-game naps. Naps can give you a temporary improvement in alertness and performance for a few hours. Naps are not a replacement for consolidated and healthy sleep at nighttime. If you're having difficulty with your sleep, you should eliminate naps." (https://www.universityofcalifornia.edu/news/how-sleep-pro-athlete)

You've got this!

I hope you've had a fun adventure so far! Keep practicing your mindset hacks and tools. Remember, the more you practice, the faster Do-It will give you what you want and deserve. And, ***you deserve to be happy.***

Also, there's so much more my team and I want to share with you... it just wouldn't fit in this book, so go to:

 TheSmilingAthlete.com
to sign up and get lots of
free new hacks and tools personally emailed to you!

Plus, you'll get first dibs on our next book, and see our list of other awesome mindset books by some great authors!

And, **please leave an honest review on Amazon** for this book, just a line or two. It would mean the world to me. I personally read each review, and your feedback really makes a difference! *Coach Bain*

 AMAZON REVIEW PAGE:
https://rebrand.ly/smilereview